ISBN 979-8-9908052-0-0 (paperback)

ISBN 979-8-9908052-1-7 (Ebook)

Authored by: Sherrie Leigh Kays

Visuals by: Sherrie Leigh Kays

Dedication

To the ones in my life who truly bring me joy.

You know who you are.

Introduction:

This book is not for the weak. It is for those who wish to work hard, get stronger, and move toward more joy and satisfaction. Real changes must be made in our lives if we truly want to claim our deserved joy. We must *intentionally* move from occasional moments of happiness to overall joy. One realization is that taking care of our own needs is not selfish, but it is necessary in order to have joy in our lives.

Hence the title, *It IS All About You.* Ultimately, this book is about shifting from moments of happiness to a more consistent state of joy. There are humorous lines in the book, but the overall meaning of the book is to find your joy, lifelong contentment.

This book contains 10 ways that I have found in working with others that help move from happiness to joy which will ultimately improve mental health and physical health, which are completely connected (maybe another book idea). I have added visuals for visual comprehension, as well, and there are pages at the end for notes and self-analysis.

Sherrie Kays 2024

It IS All About You

You

Moving from Happiness to Joy

Sherrie Leigh Kays, M.Ed. LMHC
Clinical Mental Health Counselor

Contents

Happiness or Joy?

Many of us were raised with the ideas of putting others before ourselves. However, in the grand scheme of things, this is not healthy for us. Taking care of ourselves is the only way to make sure we are healthy both mentally and physically. Not selfish – actually the opposite. It is self-fulfilling. The way we are taught to put others before ourselves is not completely explained when we are young. As adults, we must realize that taking care of ourselves IS helping out others, as well. As the old saying goes, "You cannot pour from an empty cup." Truth.

Happiness is an emotion, a state of emotion. Happiness is usually a feeling of elation, simple joy, satisfaction, and being content or fulfilled. Happiness, in general, can mean different things to different people. However, JOY described as giving oneself a feeling of positivity and overall life satisfaction. Think of it this way: Happiness happens. Joy is a choice.

Emotions are tricky. Emotions are usually short-lived. Ultimately, we do not want our happiness to be short-lived, but in fact, it is. Happiness is considered a fleeting emotion, an emotion that is the result of an event, moment, or feeling excited.

In order to have a longer, more satisfying feeling,

we should reach for joy. Joy is considered more long- term, a state of being that has long-lasting results and is usually considered as being content and satisfied. Joy is having *more constant* contentment and satisfaction with life in general. A good way to look at happiness and joy is by considering if the feelings is

circumstantial, or if the feeling defies the circumstances.

Happiness	Joy
Emotion-related Usually temporary or circumstantial Externally caused	State or condition Continual, constant, long-term Internal
	Sherrie Kays 2004

Overall, we do want happiness in our lives, but the ultimate goal is joy, as it is a state of being rather than circumstantial. We want peace in our lives that others cannot define. It is our OWN sense of joy and peace.

I think the questions to ask ourselves is "Do I want true joy,, contentment, and satisfaction in my life?" and

"What do I _need to do_ to attain joy?" Sounds easy enough. However, choosing joy is a difficult decision for many. The decision to choose joy will not make you joyous immediately. It is a long, difficult path where other choices must be made along the way. Remember, joy is a habit that is formed.

Good habits take time.

Joy is a universal language that can be understood without any words. People who experience joy recognize it, but more importantly, understand it. It does not matter what language is spoken because we usually do not have to understand the spoken word. We see joy in others. Joy is relatable notwithstanding age, culture, or ethnicity.

Joy is something we have the capacity for because it is a universal human emotion. Sometimes this is found in us daily, or we have to find it and work for it daily. Joy causes change. Sometimes, we stumble upon this change. Sometimes, we create it ourselves.

Joy changes the world around us, as well. We _attain_ joy. We _share_ the joy. It is not just nice to have joy. It is a necessity in our lives that increases our productivity, creativity, resilience, and makes us physically healthier, which is absolutely necessary for us.

Capacity for change. Change in ourselves.

Change in the world around us. Joy is universal
and possible for all of us.

Other cultures and countries give us the beauty of
the word joy in many different ways. Usually, their
joy is in the form of doing. For example, pure vida
in Costa Rica embodies prioritizing what is
important to the people *Dolce far niente* in Italy is
savoring the moment, or simply the sweetness of
nothing. There is no stress over going the extra
mile. Let life happen, do nothing, and enjoy it. In
Japan, *Wabi sabi* translates to simplicity.

Japanese enjoy the simple things in life.
Joy is achieved by accepting the imperfections
Norwegians experience *friluftsliv*. This is taking in
the natural beauty of their country – the profound
experiences of nature that need no translation.

Hearing the simple word for joy in other
languages is just an example of the universality of
the experience of joy.

This visual is presented in order to help us to
understand -- joy is universal, but not everyone
experiences joy. It is a choice we must deliberately
make in order to achieve it. It is choosing a
lifestyle that is better for you emotionally,
physically, and mentally. It is not something that
we do one day and then don't do the next. It is

purposeful each and every day. Happiness happens. Joy is choice. The difficult part of achieving joy is making a conscious decision to do so.

Joy in Other Languages

Language	Word for Joy
Spain -- Spanish	Alegría
France – French	Joie
Italy -- Italian	Gioia
Finland– Finnish	Ilo
Ireland – Irish	Áthas
Scotland – Scottish Gaelic	Gàirdeachas
Romania – Romanian	Bucurie
Greece – Greek	Χαρά
Hawaii – Hawaiian	hau'oli
Haiti – Haitian Creole	kè kontan

Sherrie Kays 2024

1

It is not your responsibility to make others happy.

Their happiness is their responsibility.

Yes, I said it!

Remember, happiness is an emotion that can come and go. True joy lies in a more consistent feeling of contentment and satisfaction. Happiness happens. Joy is a choice.

Now, this does not mean we ignore others' feelings and emotions. When others are happy, we celebrate with them. When others are grieving, we grieve with them. We are not ignoring the needs of others, but we are responsible for ourselves. This does mean that we cannot hold ourselves liable for their happiness. Happiness (and ultimately joy) is _their_ responsibility. Everyone goes through difficulties. Sharing these moments with others is a part of life. Achieving true joy means that we are not responsible for others' state of being – the joy they have or do not have. This responsibility is on them.

Part of finding joy is finding meaning in life. Pursuing meaning makes us ready for what comes our way. Happiness can be fickle and can sometimes have us questioning when circumstances arise that falter our "happiness".

There is a control factor in happiness versus joy – happiness cannot be controlled, but joy is all about control. We have control in our lives and are able to CHOOSE JOY not just moments of happiness.

We cannot control other people's feelings and emotions. Therefore, we cannot control their happiness. Sometimes we take responsibility for other people, and this is something that is out of what's known as our *Circle of Control*.

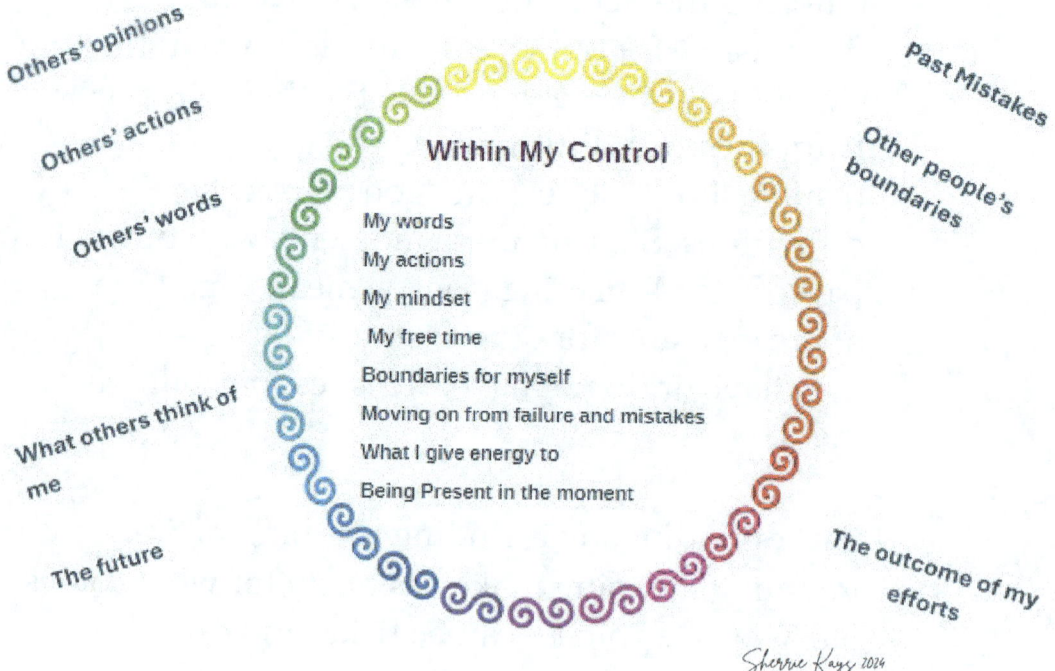

CIRCLE OF CONTROL

Outside of my control – outside the circle

Others' opinions

Others' actions

Others' words

What others think of me

The future

Past Mistakes

Other people's boundaries

The outcome of my efforts

Within My Control

My words
My actions
My mindset
My free time
Boundaries for myself
Moving on from failure and mistakes
What I give energy to
Being Present in the moment

Sherrie Kays 2024

When you study the inside of the circle, this represents you. You can see that the only things we can control are about _only_ ourselves – our words, our actions, and our mindset are well within our control. When you look at free time, boundaries, moving on, where our energy goes, and actually being present in the moment, these may be harder for us to accept control over. However, it is important for our own well-being to make sure we are in control over all of the things inside the circle. Everything outside of the circle is outside of our control. I cannot control what other people say or do. That is their responsibility. I cannot control or worry about the future. I am not a mind reader. Other people's opinions and words are out of my control. Most importantly, though, is the fact that I can control _myself_ and to whom I give time, energy, and attention. This is where we start to see joy rather than moments of happiness.

I like to think about the Circle of Control in ways that we can relate. I think of the _Serenity Prayer_. After all, doesn't serenity mean peaceful, calm, and overall untroubled?

God, grant me the serenity to accept the things I cannot change,
the courage to change the things I can, and the wisdom to know the difference.

Think about these words for a moment. When you truly consider this prayer to be used in places where people might feel out of control, it helps us learn so much. There are things we cannot change. Accept it. Move forward. There are things we can change. Courage allows us to make hard choices.

Courage through difficulty and the strength to face the hard times allows us to truly make changes.

I think the most important line in this prayer is *the wisdom to know the difference*. THIS! We have to know the difference in what we can control and what we cannot. We have to know the difference between who we choose to be and who we don't choose to be. We must realize what we want and where we want to go.

It is up to me to gain the knowledge and power to realize what is fixable and what is not, and it is up to me to move forward, keeping my serenity and joy.

2

Stop giving in to needy people.

Stop giving in to needy people – you know, the people that completely drain you both physically and mentally? I think I heard someone reference these folks as "Needy Vampires" – they suck the life out of everyone around them (physically and mentally). You may have heard these people called different things, like Energy Vampires or Emotional Vampires. No matter what we label them, these people require distance for peace.

Distancing ourselves from these Needy Vampires works out best for our own mental well- being. This is not to say we completely cut off these types of friends or family members, but distance is important. This means that we dedicate time to these people only when our mental energy can handle it.
You choose.

These needy people in our lives might not even realize they are draining the people who are trying to be a part of their lives. For instance, some are truly caught between what they think is right, good, moral, and so forth, and cannot make the decision of peace for themselves. These Needy Vampires don't want to truly solve issues. Usually, it is their job to point out issues with no solution. It is difficult to achieve joy.

Consider this conversation with a Needy Vampire:

Person 1: I really need to get my yard cleaned up and all of the cooking done for the upcoming family picnic.
Person 2: Oh, a family picnic sounds so fun!
Person 1: You should come. You could come early and help me get all set up.
Person 2: When is your picnic planned?
Person 1: Family will be getting there around noon. That's why I need you to come at 8:00 or 9:00 to help me get everything done.

Person 2 is in a spot now. Person 1 did not even ask! This person made a strong statement about _needing_ help. How could Person 2 get out of having to be at her friend's house four hours before the party? My answer might look something like this:

Person 2: Well, this family picnic is for your family. I am not sure I want to crash a family gathering.
Person 1: But, you _are_ family to everyone coming, and I really could use your help.
Person 2: I cannot be there at 8:00. I could come a little bit early and make sure you get the food on the tables.

Person 2 was sucked in to the conversation by Person 1. Person 1 is, obviously, our Needy Vampire. This was a manipulative way to invite her friend to the family picnic but to _intentionally_ try to get her to help do all the work, as well. Her neediness puts her friend's needs aside and assumes the friend will be at her beckoned called. However, setting the limits on what the Needy

Vampire could request of her kept her peace.

Consider this conversation with the Needy Vampire not actually present for the conversation but making those in his life suffer:

Person 1: I am supposed to honor my mother and father.
Person 2: Your father is very verbally abusive to you.
Person 1: He is my father! I cannot disrespect him.
Person 2: If you are going to continue to allow him to degrade and disrespect you, then you will never be able to have mental peace. You are never going to be able to truly live for yourself.
Person 1: He told me he wished I had been born a boy. Do you know how hurtful this is? He never showed up for me when I was young. He was, and still is, so mean and angry. Person 2: I cannot imagine how this must have been for you. He seems to truly have a mental hold on you, keeping you from making the best decisions for yourself. I think you may need distance because it is affecting how you are with your friends and colleagues.
Person 1: What do you mean?
Person 2: Allowing this has possibly made you strive for love and affection in negative ways. Your decision-making falters sometimes because you still want to seek his approval, and you might be seeking approval through other people -- sometimes from the wrong people and in the wrong places.
Person 1: I hear what you are saying. It is just difficult when he tells me, "I am your father!" anytime I have a different opinion than him or express something he disagrees with.
Then, the insults begin.

Person 1 has an unhealthy relationship with her father. This relationship probably led her to become emotionally attached to others in her life because of the verbal and emotional abuse she suffered as a child. The lack of emotional attachment to her father may have resulted in her need to attach to other people, reaching for what she did not get from her father. On the other hand, she is attached to the idea that her father is to be respected without question because he is her father. The disrespect and degradation from her father have held her back and caused emotional harm because she truly feels she is breaking the Biblical rule of *"Honor they father and mother."* I don't think that any higher being would want someone to suffer like this.

In the case of this unhealthy relationship, her father fits the mold of *need*. He has kept her under his control (and abuse) and manipulated her emotions. Her insecurities and fear caused her to forget that she was never really close or connected to her father because of his treatment of her. There is no happiness in trying to please those we cannot. The sooner we realize this, the better. We can honor ourselves by creating a safe, emotional space for ourselves. Doing this is not disrespectful at all!

By the way, Person 1 distanced herself from her father. She stated, "It changed me." She followed up this statement, confirming that she is now seeing her father on _her_ terms, when she is mentally capable of handling time with him. "I felt such a relief", unlike what she expected to feel. When asked about the disrespect she thought she would be giving him, she stated, "Respect is earned, and it goes both ways. I have to set the mental boundaries for myself." She also stated that when she looked back on her father and his interactions toward her, she realized that _he_ was the one not available for her emotionally.

Emotional attachment is necessary for us, but we have to have a _healthy_ emotional attachment with those around us. Healthy attachments mean that we feel close, connected, and comfortable with that person. We have confidence in our OWN abilities with that person.

I considered this for a long time, and while finishing up a session with one of my clients, I jotted down the subjects that my client and I collaborated upon in order to produce something that would stick. I created a star and labeled the five points of the star with the reasons you might need to distance yourself from Needy Vampires. I called it the _5 Points of Distance_.

Each point on the star justifies if an extremely needy person in our life might qualify for a little distance. Person 1, in the conversation about her father, found a need to create a safe space for herself – distance from her father, without disrespecting him, but gaining respect for herself.

5 Points of Distance
Distance yourself from...

People who make you
question yourself

People who
make you
feel anxious

People who
drain you
mentally

People who make you
end up feeling worse
after seeing them

People who question
your WHY

Sherrie Kays 2024

When thinking about this even further, I thought about how we could really *own* the distance. I thought of it this way: Distance means that no one has control over your mental energy. When I have a conversation with a friend or a family member, I want to leave that conversation in the same or a better mental state than when the conversation started. If you have a friend or family member that drains you just during a general conversation, it might be time to question your distance-factor. If you feel negatively when considering this, then you have answered your own question.

Toxic seems to be a word that is thrown around very freely in today's society. However, we may truly have people in our lives that do define the word toxic. Toxic people add negativity and upset the balance of your life (and usually others' lives, too). Their toxic talk define the toxic feelings that we have after giving these people our time. The only person that can define how toxicity affects you is you. Your feelings are affected by these people; therefore, you are the one that identifies these toxic emotions and feelings you are experiencing.

For a more positive association, I like to use the phrase "emotionally draining" rather than toxic because of the negative connotation the word toxic brings to mind. As previously mentioned, toxic is an overused word that sometimes doesn't truly apply to the situation. We probably have people in our lives that are emotionally draining rather than truly toxic. Choosing not to have people that add negativity and upset the balance of life can be liberating and help add joy in our lives rather than draining our own personality.

Remember how you are affected by the person – their words and actions – is a measure of how you feel. This usually is spot on about how a person affects you and affects your feelings. These people are out of our Circle of Control, but we can control ourselves and what we want to endure. Listen to your intuition and feelings regarding these types of relationships.

Think about Toxic Talk and Toxic Feelings and consider your relationships.

Toxic Talk

I really cannot believe you would consider that.

Sherrie Kays 2024

Wait! YOU got a promotion? Wow!

If you lose some weight, you will feel so much better. I did.

I'd feel guilty if I... (finish appropriately)

I could never afford to drive a ____. How do you do it?

Toxic Feelings

Drained after talking with them

Increased stress when talking with them or immediately after

Not feeling good about yourself -- lower self-confidence and lower self-esteem

Not feeling genuinely heard during conversations with them

Feeling guilty because you do things differently or have different things than they do.

Sherrie Kays 2024

This visual absolutely shows how toxicity can be physically and emotionally draining. We are the only ones responsible for putting ourselves into these situations.

3

Know where you've been.

Know where you're going.

Don't forget where you came from

But never lose sight of where you are going

Sherrie Kays 2024

Recognize mistakes. Move forward. Mistakes do not define a person. Mistakes make the person. Mistakes are proof we are trying. We have all heard probably one of these lines. In conjunction with the arrow that has to be pulled to its limit in order to soar farther, when we make those mistakes (falling backward), then hopefully, we soar to greater things (like the released arrow).

We are all imperfect. There are probably many mistakes you are thinking about right now. Don't!

Mistakes are meant as lessons – hard ones sometimes, but lessons, nonetheless. If we were all defined by our mistakes, we would be a pitiful lot.

Mistakes actually make us into the people we are. We make mistakes. We learn a lesson (usually). We grow. Bob Ross stated, "There are no mistakes – only happy accidents." This is usually true of most mistakes. However, what about those mistakes that we are still holding regret about?

Guilt is a powerful thing. Guilt over past mistakes can truly consume us if we allow it to. I think of it this way: regrets can either burden us or bless us. We have the power to choose which. We must use our mistakes to learn and move forward. It is the past, and it cannot be undone. However, we can turn these guilty thoughts around by reframing them. Think of it this way. If I reframe my thoughts into possibilities of the here and now, I have done a great job of overcoming regret and guilt.

But, what if I make the same mistake the same way I did before? The old saying goes, "Fool me once, shame on you. Fool me twice, shame on me. Fool me three times, shame on the both of us." Continual patterns of similar mistakes can lead to a vicious cycle of punishing ourselves for "always messing up." What happens then? We have to stop punishing ourselves, and we have to make *deliberate* attempts to correct. We are responsible for our mistakes. We are responsible for correcting our mistakes and moving forward. Our goal in life is not to fix our past, but it is to make the future as positive and amazing as possible.

The important thing is to make sure to recognize the mistakes as issues, giving you strength to move forward. We have to be able to admit when we have messed up and keep moving forward with the proper adjustments. This is a process, a process similar to a cycle of loss, so to speak. We have to go through a cycle of improvement with our mistakes. The cycle must include understanding of the mistake. We have to accept the mistake was made and even grieve our mistake. Until we have done this, we cannot move forward. Talking to a trusted friend or family member may help us process the mistake and move forward. The most important part of the cycle is to LEARN and move forward. If we don't learn, then we are bound to repeat. This may mean changing up parts of ourselves, so we do not keep repeating. This is okay. In fact, it is great!

There are the 3 G's I like to consider when analyzing mistakes: Grow, Get Away, and Get to Moving Forward! We must grow from the past. We must get away from the shame of our mistake. We must go forward deliberately. This can only occur after we have cycled through our mistake. This is the *Oops, I Messed Up* visual:

Oops, I Messed Up

Understand Your Mistake
Accept Your Mistake
Grieve Your Guilt
Talk to a Trusted Friend to Express Yourself
Learn from Your Mistake

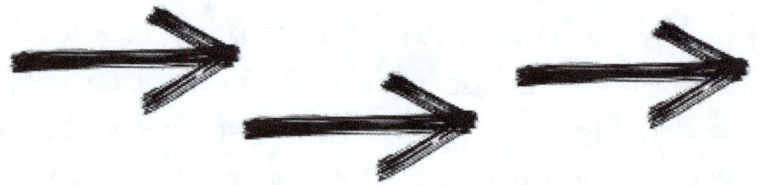

Grow from the Past
Get Away from the Shame
Get to Moving Forward -- **Deliberately**

Sherrie Kays 2024

I recently had a conversation with someone who was going through a divorce. The couple had already been separated for several months, and sometimes they lived like they were single, and sometimes they spent days at a time together. One day, the female looked at me and said, "What am I doing?". The conversation went like this:

Female: I don't understand why we are in this situation. What am I even doing at this point?
Me: Why do you think both of you are not moving forward, either with each other or without each other?
Female: I truly don't know why.

Me: If you are asking for advice, I cannot give it to you. What I can say is that you both are spending days at a time, which satisfies both of you emotionally, physically, sexually, and all the other good stuff. These days are filled with all the good things, and you are not thinking about being "separated".

Female: Yes, that is the truth. But, I love spending time with him.

Me: Neither one of you is going to make a commitment either way if one of you can come and go as you please and still have all the "good stuff".

Female: Oh wow! That makes complete sense. It's like I am giving in to all the good things, and then he goes away for a week at a time.

Me: Exactly. What do you think about that?

Female: He is getting what he wants for a few days, and then he is going on about his own life.

[pauses…a long while]

Female: I think it is a mistake to let this happen. It makes me feel used. He gets what he wants, but we never discuss the hard stuff, like fixing our marriage. You know, the day-to-day stuff.

Me: I think you should go back and really consider why you separated in the first place. Ask yourself these questions:

Do you know why?

Do you like being used, as you said?

Have you thought about a deadline for this hard conversation?

Are you truly ready for the outcome of this?

After several months of going back and forth with this same situation, this same female told me that she understood much more clearly. I asked for exactly what she understood more clearly and asked her to explain this to me.

Female: I understand why we separated. I understand that my mistake was allowing him to basically get satisfied and go for days or weeks like he had no cares in the world.
Me: So, you have a greater understanding of some of the mistakes that you both have made?
Female: I know now that we have to make a decision, and we cannot keep doing what we are doing.
[female is in tears]
Female: I set a day for basically moving out. I even made an appointment for movers. I cannot go on living like this, and he is showing no signs of really wanting to face any issues in our marriage or changing how we are living now. I have to do this for me and stop making the same mistake over and over.

Me: This sounds very intentional on your part. It sounds like you are ready to stop cycling in the mistake. It is so very hard to make a decision like this. However, you have decided on yourself. That's important. Like I said, it is not going to be easy. It may be like an emotional roller coaster for you.
Female: I have been on an emotional roller coaster for 8 or 9 months, and I am tired of feeling like this.
Me: It sounds like you are ready to move forward and keep looking in that direction.

There was more to the conversation that I will not reveal, but she admitted not to her marriage itself being a mistake, but the cycling of basically playing house for days at a time, and then allowing him to come and go as he wished being the mistake. She recognized that this may not be healthy for her, and she deliberately made the decision to move forward without him and to stop allowing his control over her by coming to the house and then leaving without contact for so long at a time. She had her *"Oops I Messed Up!"* moment and wanted change.

There is something learned from all experiences we go through. We must learn to go through life with an open mind, an open heart, and an open outlook. We must ask ourselves similar questions as were asked in this conversation:

Do I know why?
Do I want to do it again?
Am I truly ready to move on from this? What is my deadline to move on from this?

Moving Forward...Deliberately. Our mindset must be completely focused on where we are going – not where we have been. Mistakes are going to happen. If we let them continue to happen, it is not a mistake. It is a habit. Negative habits are hard to break. Therefore, deliberate action on our part must happen. Deliberate mindset must happen.

4

Stop trying to fix everything and everyone.

Guess what? There are a lot of things that are not fixable!

When we stop trying to fix everything around us, it is liberating. You will feel the change in yourself. Not everyone wants to be fixed, nor are they willing to be fixed. Stop worrying about all the little things you think you need to fix all around you. You are sucking the energy right out of yourself.

If you think you have to do this, you probably have a fixer personality that stems from your earlier years. The good news is that you can gradually release yourself from this burden of trying to fix. I have witnessed people trying to fix what doesn't need to be fixed. Man! They must be really exhausted all the time!

Think about the following conversation.

Person 1: She really needs to stop what she is doing to herself. Her drinking has cost her so much. She has lost a lot of great jobs and her family is pulling away from her because she refuses to get help.
Person 2: What do you want to do?

Person 1: I think we need to talk to her. There's got to be someone she will listen to. We need to help her get her life back together.
Person 2: And how are you going to go about this conversation? You do know she has an alcohol problem, and most of the time, there is no "fixing" another person's illness.

Person 1: We just need to help her fix her life.

While Person 1 might have good intentions, the person these two are talking about might not accept their intentions. Person 1 appears to be stepping in and feeling the NEED to change the subject of this conversation immediately. It may be hard to realize, but most people don't want to change. Usually, something drastic happens to cause a change in someone who has a drinking problem. We have to be very strong-willed in order to make hard changes in our lives. Be intentional and be deliberate in your attempts at moving forward.

Fixer personalities are everywhere. Don't cringe if you fall into this category. Remember, acts of kindness and compassion are truly admirable and desired by most of us. I would be a fixer personality, but I have to intentionally work on allowing others to rescue themselves. I have to intentionally realize when I cannot help and back away. One of the most important things we can do as a fixer is practicing our own balance and self-care. When you think about it, fixers usually neglect what they need themselves. We have to be diligent in practicing a balance of time and energy, intentionally practice self-care, and be completely honest with ourselves. Our personal time and energy has to take priority. Otherwise, we do not have the time and energy for what is most important to us – family, physical exercise, personal time, time with our spouse. We cannot neglect what is most important to us by fixing everything and everyone else.

At the forefront, taking responsibility for another's choices and actions is setting us up for disappointment, but moreover, it is allowing the other person to have ZERO motivation to change and grow themselves. We all have to face consequences for the choices we make, whether good choices or bad choices, in order to grow. If we don't allow others the opportunity to grow, these folks may never change.

Growth from happiness to joy means that we work on ourselves and allow others to do the same.

Fixer personalities want to be responsible for others and everything. This is draining! We must work on ourselves first.

The key point with a fixer personality is this:

1. There are people who HAVE to be fixers for their own reasons (which they may not realize)

2. There are people who WANT to be fixers and are driven by altruism, the act of helping others.

Both of these points show kindness and compassion for others. It is the CHOICE we make that truly shows kindness and compassion for others.

Do you feel you HAVE TO, or do you know you WANT TO?

Visualize these two types of fixers shown in the pictures:

Fixer Personalities
HAVE TO DO THIS

Overextend yourself
HAVE to feel needed
HAVE to be in control
Strong belief systems -- to a fault
NEED to fix
Don't wait for others to say "No"
NEED others to depend upon them

Fixer Personalities
WANT TO DO THIS

WANT to extend themselves to others
WANT to feel needed
Know when to relinquish control
Strong character and self-worth
WANT to fix
Accept when others say "No"
WANT others to grown and learn

Sherrie Kays 2024

As you can see from this visual, there is a difference between HAVE to and WANT to. The fixers who HAVE to do it because of a need they are experiencing are the ones who are usually interfering in others' lives. It is bothersome to the ones they feel they HAVE to fix. The fixers who WANT to do things for other people, out of the goodness of their hearts, will understand and accept when another says, "Not right now."

This brings me to a point of contention in "fixing" things. Complaining. We cannot complain without solutions to fix the problems about which we are complaining. The complainer only wants to complain most of the time and rarely offers solutions to the problems.

I recently had a conversation with a sweet young lady who has the best of intentions, but she was always complaining about how things are, what needed to change, and talked about how management should lead more at her workplace. I listened very intently -- not to say this was easy to do. I finally spoke and said, "That's a lot of problems. What are the solutions?" I think she was a little stunned.

In other words, if you have complaints, offer solutions. If you want to complain, have all the facts, and then consider solutions to put forth. Remember, your feelings and opinions don't play into facts.

Complaining is just that – complaining -- unless you have facts to back up your complaint and a proposed solution for the problem.

Griping about it and not doing anything about it will not change anything. If we are going to "fix" things, then let's fix them and stop complaining about them. Simple – provide the facts and offer solutions. Otherwise, we might become known as a miserable wretch or a Needy Vampire…maybe worse.

5

Communicate positively.

Positive communication contributes to a positive attitude. This should be easy for most of us to understand; however, sometimes conversations go wrong for whatever reason.

There are several things to consider when using positive communication – event or issue? Events can lead to issues. Let's think about this.

Events are incidents that can trigger confrontation or arguments. (The event is how the argument starts.) Things like forgetting important dates, forgetting to study for a test or forgetting to do homework, and even forgetting to call your friend back. These events sometimes cannot be controlled, but these events trigger issues if not addressed.

Issues are considered key problems in the relationship, family, or friendship. An issue is WHAT the disagreement is about. This can be everything from a lack of communication and interaction with one another to something much larger, like envy or jealousy. Consider this:

o Disagreements do not usually begin because we want conflict or discord with another.

o Those involved cannot control events that may arise, but they can control if the event becomes an issue.

How can we communicate more positively and ultimately more effectively? One of the most important communication pointers comes from a quote you have probably seen on social media, "Most people do not listen with the intent to understand; they listen with the intent to reply." There would be less dramatic reactions and more positive responses if we all listened intently and actively to the other person. Respect. Think about this. Reactions are usually negative. Responses are usually positive. With positive communication, there should be responses rather than reactions.

Many of the discussion in therapy sessions comes down to communication. I thought about effective communication after having some couple and family therapy sessions. Positive and effective communication cannot occur unless both parties are attempting this. Only one person using positive and effective communication solves very little.

Communication is important for many reasons. We all must express our wants and needs in a healthy way. If we need help, we communicate this. Usually in communication, information is given. As parties to communication, we must listen carefully and respond appropriately. One thing that proper communication does is allow us social connectedness and a closeness to those involved. It builds relationships, rapport, and builds respect. Lack of communication – in an effective and positive way – leads to distrust, lack of confidence, and strained relationships.

Effective Communication

Builds Relationship
Builds Rapport
Builds Respect   *Sherrie Kays 2024*

If communication is not doing these three things for you – building rapport, building relationships, and building respect -- then it is time to consider our ways of communication.

I like to think about it this way. If just a couple of people in your social circles began deliberately attempting better communication, then more effective and positive communication could flow into more of our social circles. It is simply consideration for others, really. I had a client relay to me that her family thought they always had the answers to any issue and that she was evidently late to the knowledge party. Really?

You cannot learn anything by always trying to be the smartest person in the room. No one knows the answers to every issue we have, and those that really believe they do are usually hurtful to others in the way they communicate.

It's the tone. It's all about the tone.

If we are attempting to make someone else look completely ignorant, then we are the problem. It's not about being right. It is about communicating effectively and positively. If we are always trying to be the smartest in the room, we are not communicating effectively and positively.

Look at the following chart for effective communication and how to enable more effective communication in your life. Truly reflect on just how good you are at effective communication. It is the how we say it and what we choose to say.

Effective Communication

1. Use "I" statements
   a. "I feel needed when you ask me to help out"
   b. "I feel discouraged when you yell at me"
   c. "I need to talk to you about something that's bothering me".
2. Actively listen, reflect, and validate the family members words
3. Clarify if necessary with positive phrasing:
   a. "I'm not sure you heard what I meant. What I meant to say was…"
   b. "I am not sure I heard you correctly. Can you tell me that again?"
   c. "Did you mean…?"
4. Take responsibility for your own contribution to the misunderstanding, but do not accept all the blame for misunderstanding.
5. Inform family members of any obstacles:
   a. "I have had a really rough day, so if I am quiet/grouchy, you know why"
   b. "School did not go like I wanted it to today, so if I am anxious/stressed/grouchy, you know why"
6. Try to look for the best in your family members. Happy =best Unhappy=worse

Sherrie Kays 2024

Effective Communication

7. Discuss negative behaviors calmly
8. Try to let your family members know you appreciate them. Hearing "thank you" is important.
9. Let your family members know if you do not like something, so behaviors are not repeated
10. Be honest with family members. Concerns should be shared, so there is no build up, resentment, and bitterness.
11. Share concerns in a positive, respectful, constructive, caring way. Negative things are usually hard to hear, so be gentle.
12. Listen actively and with acceptance when a family member has chosen to share concerns with the family. Expressed wants and needs should not be assumed as criticism.
13. Let the family know you care about what is needed and wanted. Remember, that not everything that is needed is wanted, so agreement may not happen right away.

Sherrie Kays 2024

I was having a discussion with a supervisor recently concerning effective and positive communication. There was one significant standout from this conversation. If we are wanting to "win" in any type of communication, then someone actually "loses". I asked for further clarification on this statement. The clarification: we should never go into a conversation with the mindset to win it. Conversations are meant to produce more effective communication and better understanding, not to defeat another person. For example, if he wins an argument with his wife, then she loses, and the same if she wins, then he loses. I had to think about this for a minute. Ultimately, he explained, there is not a true win in an argument because the person (that he cared about the most) lost.

To say it plainly, they both have "lost". There is now less respect, a strained relationship, and a lack of rapport or confidence in being able to effectively communicate with one another. This helped me to realize that if we are attempting to win when in this situation, someone does lose – there can be extremely hurt feelings after this. My clarification came when we concluded that you should not want to _win_ against your partner (or anyone, really) It is not about _winning_. The ultimate goal is actual conversation and effective communication _for better understanding_.

Positive communication actually wins. By wins, I mean there is effective communication between the parties. This leads to more moments of happiness and over a period of time, a more content, satisfied level of joy. With positive communication, there is relationship, rapport, and respect built with the communication.

Again, one of the most important communication points – if not the most important is remembering, "*Most people do not listen with the intent to understand; they listen with the intent to reply*". It goes back to making sure the other person feels they are understood, not fixed, but understood. Positive communication usually lends itself to positive outcomes, moving toward joy and contentment.

Positive Communication

Respect for others
Actively listen
Use "I" statements
Be specific with points
Don't generalize & associate with everything
Speak one at a time (active listening)
Listen to understand not respond
Clarify when needed
Validate others' issues
Give positive feedback
Consider compromise
Admit fault when wrong and sincerely apologize

Negative Communication

Name-calling
Ignoring
Blaming
Sarcasm
Generalizing
Using superlatives, like "always" or "never"
Winning
Gloating over winning
Mind-reading
Responding without thought
Threatening words or actions

Sherrie Kays 2024

6

Be honest with yourself.
Assess yourself. Manage yourself.

This is a tough one. Being honest with yourself, assessing yourself, and then managing yourself can be more than we want to even consider. Let's ponder each one and how each statement can lead to more fulfillment and ultimately the joy we are trying to achieve.

Be Honest With Yourself. Some of you may be thinking, "I don't even know what this means?" Being
honest with ourselves unlocks our vulnerabilities, truly opening our eyes to who we really are. Honesty about our own vulnerabilities and weaknesses actually make us stronger than those who have no clue (or don't want to admit) what their weaknesses really are. Those who are not honest with themselves are usually insecure and show it by having to be the smartest, the prettiest, the most handsome, and so forth. This is a false belief (and a false reality) of the person. They try extra hard for attention on their "positive" characteristics because they do not want others to see their vulnerabilities and weaknesses. Admitting our weaknesses and showing our vulnerabilities demonstrate a more genuine self

and project an even better person to others, giving us an unrealized sense of peace and security within ourselves.

However, how are we to be honest with others when we are not honest with ourselves? I expect honesty of other people. I consider it absolutely necessary. The best question to ask is simple, "Am I being honest with _myself_?" As I dug deeper into what being honest with myself truly meant, I understood. This means I need to learn to accept myself for who I am. I am not perfect. This is an impossible reach for all of us. I am perfectly flawed, perfectly imperfect, and I know this. We have to know our weaknesses. This, actually, can make us stronger and more accountable.

Assess Yourself. Many of us are naive to where we need improvement. Without self-awareness, this can lead to not knowing what we are doing wrong. Therefore, improvement is next to impossible (or it is just serendipitous).

A case in point, for example, could be a rookie on the job or new parents. (Unfortunately, it does not always have to be a rookie!) These are just examples, as I have personally seen some people in varying professions (and I consider motherhood a profession all its own) that would do the same things.

- A rookie police officer who has no realization of the fact that she is responsible for the safety of thousands of community members and continues just to patrol certain areas.

o A rookie teacher (or even multi-year teacher) who has no idea that his classroom management is not up to par.

o A rookie parent does not realize that when the baby is crying, the baby needs something, food, comfort, etc.

o A rookie guidance counselor who tries to give advice rather than collaborating with the student on the best possible solutions to problems.

Each of these could show that it would be really easy to make an excuse in these scenarios if something went wrong. Being honest allows each individual to identify their own weaknesses and seek support in the identified weak areas. If I learn my weak areas, I learn to strengthen these areas rather than ignoring the facts and not taking responsibility for myself. Honesty would allow for a more 'no excuses' attitude from the person, and then accept assistance could support them. Now from the honest point of view:

o Rookie police officers realizes after talking with other officers that she is not truly covering all areas in the community. Then, she makes the decision to work more in her neglected areas to see if she can help more people in the community.

o Rookie teacher (or multi-year teacher) with classroom management issues realizes that he needs more training on how to effectively manage his classroom and seeks out this training support from administration or a trusted fellow teacher.

o Rookie parent considers why the baby is crying so much. Rookie parent talks with other mom friends and realizes that usually baby's cry for a reason.

o Rookie guidance counselor realizes after attending a clinical staff meeting that he is doing more talking in session than active listening. Rookie guidance counselor educates himself with training on attentiveness to task and active listening in order to improve while benefiting his students the most.

It is difficult for most people to be completely honest with themselves. We like to cover our flaws, rather than admit we have them. Strength is admitting to ourselves where we need work and then moving forward to manage the work needed for growth. The only way to be honest with ourselves is to be aware of our strengths and weaknesses.

Manage Yourself. Honesty with ourselves can make us very vulnerable because we may give ourselves the idea that we are weak. However, we expect others to give us honesty. Why not set the expectation for ourselves with ourselves? The strength in self-honesty comes from realizing how much stronger we can be with improvement in these weak areas. This should motivate us to better understand ourselves and improve ourselves. When we are honest with ourselves, we can begin to assess where we need work (our weak areas). Recognition is important.

Feigning strengths or knowledge only makes people look weaker and actually <u>be</u> weaker people.

This is how we learn to manage ourselves – we have to be very self-aware in order to make true change. For example, I can be completely honest with myself if I am low on energy or if my mood is lower than I want it to be. When I am completely honest about myself, I can protect both myself and others by keeping my distance, not wanting to transfer my own emotions or situation to someone else, and therefore work on my own mental health.

Honesty with Self

Knowledge of Weak Areas
Allowing Vulnerability
No Excuses Mindset
Seeking Guidance or Assistance in Weak Areas
Continual Improvement in Weak Areas

Dishonesty with Self

Ignorance or Oblivious of Weak Areas
Not Making Corrections to Self
Feigning Strength or Knowledge
Excuses!
Will Not Ask for Help
Weak Areas Could Worsen

Sherrie Kays 2024

Think about these questions when reflecting upon the honesty with yourself:

- What goals do I have?
- What will help me gain strength in my weak areas?
- What would bring me joy in my life?

Usually, answering these questions come with analyzing our strengths and weaknesses. Therefore, we must be completely honest with this introspection, searching deep within our soul for what we need improvements on.

Strengths Top 3 Things I am good at	Weaknesses Top 3 Things I need help with
1.	1.
2.	2.
3.	3.

Sherrie Kays 2024

7

Do not compare yourself to other people.

After our self-honesty journey, then we really are able to be our truer selves rather than what we <u>think</u> we should be. This means no more comparing ourselves to other people. Everyone is different.

When considering how we, as a society, are always comparing ourselves to others, I reflected back upon the *Serenity Prayer:*

God, grant me the serenity to accept the things I cannot change,
the courage to change the things I can, and the wisdom to know the difference.

Serenity. Courage. Wisdom. Key words that stand out when I returned to the *Serenity Prayer.* There are things I cannot change. There are things I can change. I have to be wise enough to know the difference. We are not here to compare ourselves to others – their house, their cars, their bank accounts. The mindset must be "Who do I want to truly be?"

I am who I <u>choose</u> to be. Other people's opinion about me is not in reality who I am. Remember, opinion is in the eye of the beholder. Facts are not. We cannot control other people's opinion (*Circle of Control*). However, we can control ourselves and the opinion we have of ourselves. This requires a great deal of self-awareness, self-confidence, and honesty.

I look at it this way. Other people's opinions and judgments do not change who I am; it reflects who they really are.

We are all different for a reason. It would be really boring if we all looked the same, talked the same, acted the same and had all of the same things. There is always going to be someone prettier/more handsome, skinnier, smarter, or that has a better car or bigger house. The sooner we accept this, the better we are as our own person. There is always going to be someone with a bigger house, more awesome car, or that has a bigger bank account.

That. Is. Okay.

We have to be satisfied with what we are doing in our own life to be content and joyful. A good way I remember -- an envious heart (which is where this comes from) is the sign of a small, unopened mind.

Someone's jealousy can consume <u>them</u>, but it has <u>no effect or impact on me</u>!

Now know, there is a difference between admiring what someone has and when we would do anything to "keep up with the Joneses." There is admiration and then there is envy. Envy is an emotion that is natural. But are we handling envy in a healthy way? We cannot allow envy to strip us of our joy. This is a good clarification question: Is it envy or admiration? Ask yourself these questions for self- awareness, especially when envious thoughts creep in.

Answer honestly.

o   *What does Sally have that makes me feel less?*
o   *Why does it make me feel this way?*
o   *Would what Sally has fill emptiness for me?*
o   *Do I really want what Sally has at the price of my joy and peace?*

If "yes" was answered to any of these questions, we have to ask ourselves if it is worth it to have what Sally has. Honestly answer these questions for better clarification:

o   *How much will it cost me physically, emotionally, and/or financially?*
o   *Is it filling an emptiness in me?*
o   *Will I feel like a better person with the end results?*

I don't know about you, but really considering these questions and the answers made me feel like Sally can just do Sally, and I can work on myself.

I had a conversation with a young lady about this subject.

Young Lady: She has everything! Her house is so big, and it even has a pool in the back. I just wish I could have a house that big WITH a pool. Plus, she always has herself fixed in the most perfect way! She has great

clothes and shoes. Have you seen her car?
Me: I really don't know what her house looks like. I have never spent time there.
Young Lady: It has to be the biggest house around here!
Me: Sounds like she is very fortunate to be able to have a house, a pool, nice car, and nice clothes. Wow. That is a lot to be grateful for.
Young Lady: It has to be the biggest house around here!
Me: Sounds like she is very fortunate to be able to have a house, a pool, nice car, and nice clothes. Wow. That is a lot to be grateful for.
Young Lady: I bet she takes all of it for granted. She's probably in debt up to her eyeballs!
Me: Well, I don't know anything about all of that. I have enough to take care of just taking care of myself.
Young Lady: [doesn't respond]
Me: I guess that's something to consider when you are looking at her "things".

More of this conversation happened, yet the young lady did not seem to understand that she was experiencing envy – wanting what someone else has, judging someone for what they have, appearing upset because someone has something she does not. Envy can be all consuming for the one experiencing it. It is a very negative emotion.

When thinking about how to work on this issue, we should really (and honestly) look at this particular question: *Is it Envy or Admiration?* I did not hear anything in the conversation above about being proud of the other person. I did not hear anything in the conversation above about the hard work of the person who has a nice house and car. These are truly envious statements made without basis and show judgment of the other person. Admiration shows pride for another, recognition for another, and is a positive emotion.

We should try to move toward admiration, as a more positive quality. Admiration is realization of another's strengths and praising them for those strengths rather than trying to tear them down out of envy . I have seen envy really destroy people. It truly eats away at our happiness -- much more, our joy.
Joy does not come out of jealousy and envy, and we will have very little moments of true happiness with an envious heart and mind. Think of it this way. You have
heard the saying, "Green with envy", I'm sure. Envy is a monster, a green monster. Monsters usually destroy.

Look at the difference between Envy and Admiration in this visual. Envy is The Green Monster. Admiration is The Pink Pacifist.

Envy
The Green Monster

Doesn't celebrate or isn't happy when others' succeed

Judging what others do

Happy when other's fail or have setbacks

Upset when others get praise for accomplishments

Fake compliments

Trying to copy or compete with those who are the object of their envy

Spread false information or rumors

Downplays others' successes

Sherrie Kays 2024

Admiration
The Pink Pacifist

Encourages &
celebrates others'
success

Encourages others
to be better

Does not strive to
beat or compete

Happy to see
others succeed -
celebrates with
them

No drama or
falsities

Does not feed
gossip or falsities

Praises another's
accomplishments

No judgment of
others

Encourages those
who have failure or
experience set
backs

Sherrie Kays 2024

Which color are you? Are you the Green Monster,
or are you the Pink Pacifist?

If you recognize anything from the Green
Monster in yourself, reflect upon yourself, your
thoughts and your actions that cause this beast
within you. I would rather be labeled a pacifist
than a monster!

8

Set Boundaries and do not let those boundaries be broken by anyone.

Boundaries in our lives help us determine what is okay and what is not okay. Everyone needs boundaries in their lives. We can say we have them, but do we keep our boundaries strong? Do we let some people break our boundaries because of who they are in our lives? Honestly, those closest to us should respect our boundaries the most. On the other hand, those that are closest to us tend to break our boundaries and our peace pretty often. Holding our boundaries strong does not show weakness. This shows the strength of our character.

Boundaries should determine what we want and do not want to be involved with. Setting boundaries should be a priority in order for us to maintain our sense of peace and serenity. There are certain matters that must be established as a hard line that does not get crossed. This is not disrespectful to those in our lives. It shows respect for ourselves. Most of the time this helps when we need to say no. We can learn to say no respectfully. Moreover, when we say yes, it is truly meant. Boundaries keep us out of the resentment area and keep us ready and willing to give an honest answer to someone.

The way I think of boundaries is that they are a form of self-love and recognition of what we are mentally (and maybe physically) able to handle at the time. It is one of the highest forms of self-respect.

Setting healthy boundaries will allow an understanding and acceptance of who we are, who we want to be, and all the while build a sense of trust, safety, and respect in relationships. We must respect ourselves before others will respect us. It starts with us. It IS about you.

So, how do we start setting (and maintaining) boundaries if we have struggled with this or haven't had them before? We, again, must assess ourselves -- what type of person do we want to be, and what type of people do we want in our lives?

Setting boundaries begins with our most important priorities. We may have to sit down and make a priority list. Listen to your heart when making your priority list and be completely forthright about what YOU need to be more at peace in your life.

The boundaries fall only on us, as we must assume responsibility for what we know we want or need. Saying NO is necessary, but it can be done respectfully. "I cannot handle anything more right now." Do not apologize for putting yourself ahead of what others WANT when this is something you NEED. We have to be consistent with establishing these boundaries, and we must communicate why we need them.

Others do not need a detailed explanation of why. Our answer can simply be, "I have to slow down a little right now." We have to be consistent with establishing these boundaries, and we must communicate why we need them.

Others do not need a detailed explanation of why. Our
answer can simply be, "I have to slow down a little

right now." Knowing that we are setting our own boundaries around our own personal preferences is staying true to ourselves and respecting our OWN preferences. I completely respect that someone realizes their energy is off, or that they are not having a good day, and that person takes time because they do not want to lower others' moods or energy. Communicate this.

Knowing that we are setting our own boundaries around our own personal preferences is staying true to ourselves and respecting our OWN preferences. I completely respect that someone realizes their energy is off, or that they are not having a good day, and that person takes time because they do not want to lower others' moods or energy. Communicate this. This is a very real and very honest situation we sometimes find ourselves in. How can someone dispute the fact that you realize that YOU need to slow down? They don't get to attempt to predict the feelings you are having or the physical drain you may feel.

Consider the benefits of setting boundaries in your life. There are clear benefits to setting boundaries and keeping those boundaries.

Benefits of Boundaries

Greater autonomy and confidence
Clear expectations for others
Decreases stress and anxiety
Improves emotional health
Improves relationships
Lessens burnout
Self-respect and respect from others
Time needed for YOU

Sherrie Kays 2024

Look at all of that positivity and the benefits to a better you! Can you imagine how much better we all would feel with clear boundaries? It is completely part of self-care and mental health awareness -- to set boundaries of protection. Boundaries allow us to be mindful of balancing life. Boundaries allow us to choose our health and well-being , allowing time for our own hobbies, interest, and much needed self-care.

One of the topics I discuss with my clients is

social media. Yes, social media is a part of boundaries. We have to create a less stressful interaction with social media because social media plays a huge role in our day-to-day lives. Social media has its positives and negatives. I discuss the need for not being so tied to your phone that you are missing out on the wonderful things around you.

I prefer to set my social media to "notifications off" to have more peace throughout the day. Not only does this limit me, but it also prevents increased anxiety and stress over the constant need to check the incoming messages and posts.

We have discussed setting boundaries for ourselves, but what does it look like when someone is not respectful of our personal space? This can occur if we have not made our boundaries clear, or it can be that the person is completely ignoring our boundaries and disrespecting those boundaries.

The following situation popped into my head when I was considering discussing boundaries and how people try to break our boundaries:

Friend 1: Cassie called me and wants to get coffee and catch up.
Friend 2: Why would you have coffee with her when you and I haven't had coffee in weeks…maybe months?
Friend 1: I have not seen her for a while. We have barely texted in the last month.
Friend 2: She must want something, then. Friend 1: Why would you think that?
Friend 2: She always calls you instead of me. I need my bestie time with you.

Friend 1: Why don't we get together later this week?
Friend 2: Well, this week, you have Cassie. You could just cancel and hang out with me.
Friend 1: We can go later in the week. I have already set plans with Cassie.

Friend 2 is trying to make Friend 1 feel guilty about having coffee with Cassie instead of her. This is a form of manipulation that comes from a deeper place inside Friend 2. This is a way to breach boundaries with those we feel close to. Friend 2 absolutely wants to penetrate the boundaries that Friend 1 has established for herself. Friend 1 does not want to break her coffee date with Cassie because she *wants* to see her. Friend 2 is attempting to cross the boundaries Friend 1 has – not allowing others to manipulate her or delegate who she can spend time with and who she can't.

Does this type of conversation sound familiar? If it does, you may have a friend that manipulates you into feeling guilty for not spending all your time with him/her. First, this is unacceptable behavior. Second, it crosses a personal line. Friends should never manipulate their friends to get their way or to attempt to keep them solely to themselves. This is very unhealthy and negative behavior. Moreover, guilt trips by others should not cause you to give up your peace of mind. Maintain your sense of peace. This is not on you. It is about the friend's behavior.

Think of this situation:

Friend 2: Why did you tell me that your mom came over to your house?
Friend 1: I did not realize I needed to tell you that.
Friend 2: You told me that your son was sick. You told me that he had fever.
Friend 1: Well, Mom called to check on him. I told her his fever broke, and she offered to bring us some lunch.
Friend 2: I would have done that if you would have let me know.
Friend 1: I did not know until my son's fever broke. Then, Mom called to check on him, offering food.
Friend 2: I cannot believe you would let her come over after you told me he was sick!
Friend 1: I understand this might look suspicious to you, but in reality, it was just a coincidence. I hope you understand. More importantly, she is my son's grandmother and wanted to give him some love.

Wow! If you have a friend that reacts like this, RUN – RUN AWAY FAST! This is not a friendship. Sounds like a dictatorship. To give you an example of the aftermath -- Friend 1 completely shut out Friend 2 for this happenstance. Does this conversation and situation sound familiar? May I say this was a _grandmother_ stepping in to help out her grandson and her daughter. Friend 2 did not hear from Friend 1 for weeks. This is also a form of manipulating another's boundaries and attempting to give out guilt and isolation as punishment. **RUN AWAY.**

This is a friend who tries to make the other feel guilty. First, there was absolutely no reason to behave in this manner. This is a manipulative way for the friend to make you feel guilty for excluding them, when in reality, no one was excluded. Only in Friend 1's mind was she excluded. Again, This is not on you. It is about the friend's behavior. Second, the household had sickness in it. Enough said. Third, the person who came was the grandmother of the sick little one. I think there is enough said on that, too.

This is another way that people close to us want us to give in and break our boundaries. Finding guilt. There was a boundary established in order to maintain peace in a sick household – both for the sick child and for the mom who probably needed rest, as well. The mom should not feel guilty for how the other person reacts in this case. This type of reaction is on the other person.

Both of these scenarios show not only an attempt to break another's boundary, but an example of a Needy Vampire (Chapter 2). Why would either of these scenarios make a difference to the manipulator (one attempting to make the other feel guilty) for not

including her? It makes no sense. The first scenario: she was not invited. The second scenario: there was a sick child, and the grandmother stepped in to help her daughter and grandson.

Neither of these situations should make us feel guilty for setting and maintaining boundaries. In this situation, the boundaries must be maintained in order to maintain a sense of peace. Otherwise, this "friend" could mentally drain the other. May I give a little reminder -- unfortunately, there are not just friends that may do this to us. It could be our own family members who try the guilt trip trick. You may not be able to run away from family, but you do not need to give in to this manipulation tactic.

Let's talk about the obvious in some situations – co-dependency. Situations requiring boundaries may come in the form of another person's co-dependency issues -- needing another person because he/she struggle to maintain his/her own identity or independent choices.

Another part of co-dependency is an excessive reliance on one another for justification of self-worth and emotional well-being. Boundaries tend to be crossed because of enabling this unhealthy habit. When someone does not respect your boundaries, it is an invasion of privacy. You may even feel violated in some way. This may lead the boundary violator to use manipulative tactics to control the situation, like guilting you to get their way or attempting to control your emotions, thoughts, or actions by making comments about you. All of these types of violations are a sign of disrespect toward you and ultimately shows weaknesses in the violator.

Remember, you are not responsible for others' weaknesses. Remember, you are not responsible for others' happiness. They must seek out happiness and find joy on their own.

True joy won't come from another person but within us.

We saw some of the positive benefits of setting our boundaries. Let's consider what healthy boundaries ARE NOT:

Healthy Boundaries are not...

Emotional manipulation or guilt tripping to get their way

Giving in because you are concerned about hurting another's feelings

Relying on others for sense of self-worth, meaning, or personal identity

Invading personal space and privacy -- lack of respect

Sherrie Kays 2024

In Chapter 2 when we discussed needy people. Boundaries allow us to stop giving in to needy people. People that completely drain you both physically and mentally require boundaries. No question. End of discussion. These needy people might not even realize they are draining the people who are trying to be a part of their lives; therefore, communicating your boundaries will help prevent this physical and mental drain. One of my personal boundaries is to not allow others to add negativity or upset the balance of my life. I moved so quickly from happiness to joy! We cannot allow ourselves to be affected by others' poor decisions or behavior, especially if they attempt to make us feel guilty or manipulate us into being involved more in their lives. Other people should not have this kind of effect on us. We have to think of ourselves. It IS all about you in this case.

Key Points:
<u>No one</u> has control over your mental energy but you.
<u>No one</u> decides what you put up with but you.
<u>No one</u> gets to dictate your time.
<u>Not on you</u> -- This is not on you. It is about the friend's behavior or the family member's behavior.

9

Unhappy people want everyone around them to be unhappy.

Exceptionally unhappy. This usually means misery. Misery for the exceptionally unhappy person **and** misery for those around this exceptionally unhappy person. I call it the *Cycle of Misery* (see visuals in this chapter).

Unhappy people want everyone around them to share in their unhappiness. I'm miserable, so you need to be miserable with me. This is completely the opposite of the positivity we gain from choosing our joy. Unhappy people do not focus on improving their situation. They tend to continue to wallow in their own misery. Moreover, these unhappy people struggle with healthy relationships. Instead, they wish to use this time to make others feel miserable as well.

There are usually stereotypes that go with miserable people. They compete with everyone. They are always negative. They have no idea they are insecure. They want everyone to join in their "misery" (even if they don't know they are miserable or know why they are miserable.)

Usually exceptionally unhappy people see

everyone else as competition. Also, exceptionally unhappy people harm their relationships with some of the people closest to them because of their self- entitlement. In other words, *"What can you give me?"* attitude. This is somewhat of a game to the miserable.

The miserable expect others to sacrifice for them, and they will do everything to gain this expected sacrifice. Entitlement. Their entitlement is a must-win for them. For example, the miserable have to "one-up" those around them. The constant competitiveness with others, even if they don't realize they are in competition mode, is what drives them because they do not recognize their own misery. When they lose a "competition" with another person, this only adds to their negative emotions. It is a vicious cycle for the miserable person.

Unfortunately, when miserable people get filled with all of their negative emotions, they become hateful to those around them; therefore, trying to steal others' joy. No one can be happy unless I am happy, and I am not, so here's a dose of misery for you. Usually, these folks are not fully aware that this is happening because, for them, it happens all the time, but it is happening, all the same. Miserable people want their "circle" to despise the people they despise. "I hate them, so you have to hate them with me!" I really have heard this before. I had an acquaintance that once told me if one person in their family despises a person, then everyone in the family despises that particular person. This is the epitome of I hate, so you hate. What?!

Usually those who are dealing misery to others are very insecure about themselves. No matter how hard they try, they are unable to boost their own self-esteem and love themselves, and they need others to assist them with this void. Demeaning others is a way to deal with their own insecurities. Putting others down helps them feel really good (which is usually only very short-term). Let's face it, a miserable person is way beyond unhappy. Have you heard of the term "miserable wretch?" A miserable person is absolutely wretched to themselves, to others, and to the situation they may find themselves in.

In dealing with those who are chronically unhappy, we have to make sure we deal with the behavior appropriately. What does this mean? We have to protect ourselves and our own peace. Situations like the following are usually intentionally set up by the exceptionally unhappy.

Unhappy Person: I just don't think I can make it to the store today. I have such a terrible migraine. I haven't gotten to take my medicine.
Me: Oh, please let me help. What do you need from the store? Can I bring you soup or something to help? I have a meeting this afternoon. I have to pick up my kids by 5. It shouldn't take long to bring you what you need.

NO! This is exactly what the person wants from you. You are enabling the person every single time you give in to their neediness. You offer your help. You go to the store. You end up at their house consoling the person, giving them their much-needed attention. just to find out this may be exactly what this person WANTED, not what they NEEDED. NO! Let's not forget that you ran yourself ragged doing this.

This is where a person's cycle of misery thrives. If she knows she has a migraine, then she needs to immediately try to prevent it rather than "needing" someone else. The cycle of misery is shown in her not taking her prescribed medication and using the friend to "rescue her". This is classic attention-seeking behavior from a needy person.

Let's look at a response to this that could put you in a better position to protect yourself from this situation. If this intentional attention-seeking behavior has previously occurred, then we should not give-in to this cycle.

Unhappy Person: I just don't think I can make it to the store today. I have such a terrible migraine.
Me: Have you taken your migraine medication?
Unhappy Person: No.
Me: You were given this medication for this reason. You are supposed to take your medication when you feel an oncoming migraine .
Unhappy Person: I just wanted to see if it would go away first.
Me: Take your medication. Hopefully, you will feel better and be able to make it to the store. I am swamped myself, so I won't be able to get to the store and bring you anything this afternoon. I hope you get control of the migraine. Feel better soon.

This is not abandoning. Those with a good heart would think this cruel; however, it is cruel to subject ourselves to this type of attention-seeking behavior over and over again.

This type of behavior empowers the exceptionally unhappy to pay attention to _themselves_ instead of relying on others' attention. We have to end the vicious cycle that these people put us in if we do not want to end up in a miserable situation ourselves. It has a great deal to do with setting the boundaries we reviewed in Chapter 8.

Review what it takes to properly set boundaries and to distance yourself from the cycle of misery that others may be wallowing in. The less you respond to their every demand, the more peace you have in your own life.

You may be wondering how we can tell if a person is miserable and seeking out others. Miserable, exceptionally unhappy people usually have specific personality traits.

How To Tell If a Person Is Miserable

Complaining or pointing out negative side
Unfriendly
Fishing for compliments
NEEDING others' attention
Pessimistic Attitude
Anger over the little things & showing anger
Loneliness that they may not even recognize
Feeling of hopelessness or feigning abilities
Ignoring those around them

Sherrie Kays 2006

Sound familiar?

Not only do we need to stop this cycle, but we need to stop those who <u>cause</u> this cycle and empower them to do for themselves. It's a huge feat because those that are in the cycle probably have done this for so long that they cannot enable themselves easily. Give them their power back! Use your own empowerment to give them the gift of empowerment. If we don't empower those who really need it, the cycle of misery has now spread to us.

The following are examples of the Cycle Of Misery that others sometimes put us in in order for us to join in their misery.

Cycle of Misery

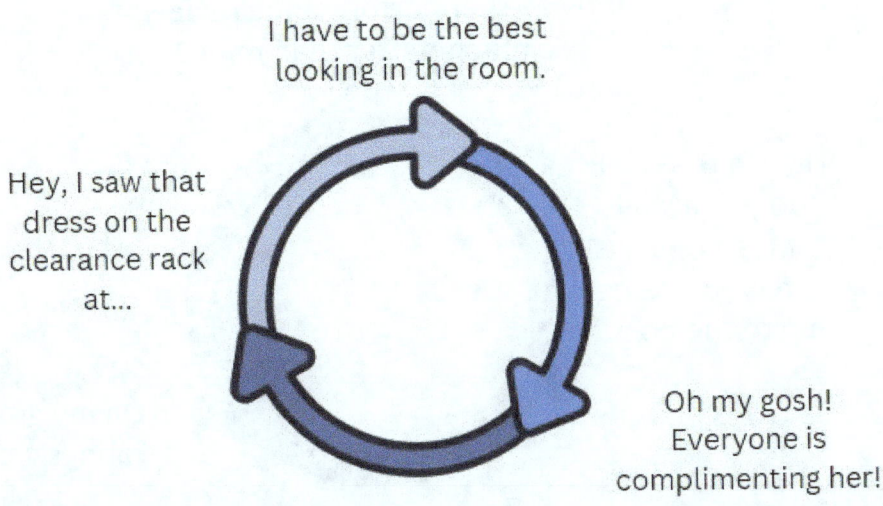

I have to be the best looking in the room.

Hey, I saw that dress on the clearance rack at...

Oh my gosh! Everyone is complimenting her!

Fishing for compliments and downgrading others when you don't receive the compliments wanted

Sherrie Kays 2024

This situation comes about more than we realize. There is so much effort within those who are exceptionally unhappy to exceed everyone else that cruel statements are made to downgrade others when they do not receive the compliments and attention they seek. Who cares how much was spend on the dress?

Cycle of Misery

Why are her performance reviews
so much better than mine?

How in the world
do you always
get high reviews?
Are you kissing
up to the boss?

Oh my gosh! Her
ratings were high
again!
Unbelievable!

Envy of another's success and
downplaying their success

Sherrie Kays 2024

Comparing ourselves to others is a tragic flaw.

When we begin to question others' abilities and
downplay others' success, it is a sign of being
miserable.

Cycle of Misery

I'm feeling awful today because
I did not take my migraine medication.

I knew you would
come and help
me feel better.

Calls on friend for
help

Gaining attention however they must and taking
advantage of others' generosity

Sherrie Kays 2024

When someone's illness is true, they will not
intentionally put themselves in the position of
getting a migraine. Migraines are a chronic
illness in which many suffer on a daily basis.
This is intentionally gaining attention and taking
advantage of others' attention. The attention
must be focused on the one who is "suffering" in
this scenario.

Distance yourself from those who insist on being miserable, especially if the exceptionally unhappy want to remain exceptionally unhappy and are not attempting change. Remind yourself of what you read in Chapter 2 and in Chapter 8. Misery is needy, hence, needy people may fall into the miserable category. Boundaries help keep you protected from falling into the traps of these people. Remember, the less you respond to their every demand, the more peace you have in your own life. This is not a cruelty to others, it is giving them the power of self-reliance.

Keep your joy and your peace intact!

10

Stop hanging around with those filled with hate.

Touchy subject, I know. This chapter will probably step on some people's toes, and that is okay. Sometimes, things have to be said regarding the touchy subject of
hate.

If you don't understand what I am talking about, then listen carefully to how others talk and act around you. Pay special attention to comments made about those who are different than the commenter. Hate is not okay.

Consider the following:

o If someone makes a "joke" about another race or ethnicity, not okay.
o If someone tells you that you cannot be friends with someone because "their family isn't good enough", not okay.
o If someone comments about "those kind of people", "they don't belong here", or says something like "that's all they know how to do", not okay.

If someone makes you feel uncomfortable when they talk about these subjects, or any type of subject, this is not okay. Distance yourself. Better yet, speak up. There is a

way to be conversational and not confrontational; however, usually closed-minded, hate-filled people cannot be bargained with.
Remember, we cannot fix everyone, nor is it our responsibility to do so. It IS all about you in this case. Protect your peace. Protect your joy.

I have always tried to look at scenarios like the ones above like this:

o Why is a person's race or ethnicity so bothersome for you?
o What defines "good enough" when talking about who I can hang around with?
o Who are "those kind of people" anyway? What's so bad about "those people"?

The United Nations defines hate speech as "*offensive discourse targeting a group or an individual based on inherent characteristics (such as race, religion, or gender) and that may threaten social peace*". Hate threatens peace. Protect your peace. Protect your joy.

If I remember history correctly, the United States is an entire country based on immigrants back to the 1600's immigrants settling in the Northeast. So, we probably are not all that different. Some may talk differently. Yes, some may look different. But, we all have to live together in a peaceful way. I don't have the energy to give to hating.

Hate is one of the most powerful words that results in powerful actions. These actions are directed at others. Hate is all about power and control, and when someone does not feel in control, hate is the easy way out. The way most people, who are really out of control, feel more in control is by hate. The haters need power and control over others. Usually this comes in the form of those that are different– for whatever reason. The hater defines the difference. History shows us that through the years, certain people took power over others who were not "up to standards". Hence the hater defines the standards and the differences of others.

This brings me to a point. Who is setting these standards for others to live up to? Shouldn't I get a say in my own standards? I thought we were all here to love and care for each other, not judge people who are different than we are. Keeping others on our hate list means we are intentionally keeping those we hate beneath us – bias, prejudice, discrimination, and even acts of violence come from hate. Usually hate is unfounded. Hate is the opinion of the beholder. I wonder if these hate-filled people have ever considered their words and actions or how they would feel if they were the target of such unfounded hatred? We have to set standards for ourselves and be able to stand by our standards. This is a difficult topic to even consider, I know.

Consider the visual and how hatred forms from unfounded opinions.

Hatred comes from unfounded opinions of...

Age
Religion
Political Affiliation
Skin Color
Gender Identity
Sexual Orientation

Sherrie Kays 2024

By unfounded opinions, this means the hater is uneducated about what they hate or misinformed by what they hate, possibly both. One of the best ways to combat hate is with education and vetted information. Not everything you read on the internet is true. Shocker! Not all news outlets on television report using unbiased words and information. Shocker! We have to be smart enough to dig for our own information, do our own research before coming to conclusions regarding others. This information has to be in an unbiased form. Searching for truth is a good way to prevent falling into hate.

Fear. Fear is usually what causes these responses in haters. Fear of the unknown. If I don't know much about someone who is different than me, then I am the one in the wrong if I chose to remain in the hate that I cannot name. We all must educate ourselves as much as possible in order to prevent this type of hatred. We must ask ourselves the hard question of "Why?" Why do we burden ourselves by hating someone else? Why am I giving so much energy to this? We must also truly question where we are getting our information. Is it family? Is it friends? News? The question really is "Have we done our own research into the information?" -- true unbiased research. Hate is a vicious four-letter word. Educate yourself. Don't allow yourself to spread hate.

Do you know that hatred affects our bodies? Our bodies suffer when we continually carry hatred. The attendees heard words at George H.W. Bush's funeral, *"Hatred corrodes the container it's carried in."* That's our bodies – that's the container! Significant physical health problems result in long-term hatred of others, not to mention the impact on our emotional health. We must separate ourselves from those who appear to thrive on hating.

Many never realize the hate they carry. Confucius told us, "If you hate a person, then you are defeated by them." Let this sink in. Who is the smaller person? Those who carry the hate or those who are hated?

Key Points:

Hatred is good for no one – the giver or the receiver. Hatred is for those who do not know better due to lack of educating themselves or an unwillingness to learn more.
Remember the key questions posed earlier:

o Why is a person's race or ethnicity so bothersome for you?

o What defines "good enough" when talking about who I can hang around with?

o Who are "those kind of people" anyway? What's so bad about "those people"?

If we don't have an educated response to these questions or any facts to support the WHY, then we are the ones in the wrong.

Summary

Always keep in mind, it is not your responsibility to make others happy. Their happiness is based on them. Not your responsibility. Find your joy!

Needy people do not need any more attention. Remember, these Needy Vampires will suck the life out of you both physically and emotionally. Make goals for yourself and do not allow anything to hinder you from those goals.

Make sure you accept your past, especially learning from your mistakes, and move forward deliberately.
We cannot fix everything and everyone. Remember, there is a difference between _have to_ and _want to_. Wanting to is fine, as long as you do not overextend yourself.

Communication must be effective and positive and not seek to "win". Remember, if you either party seeks to win, the other loses – loss of respect, rapport, and loss of relationships. Effective and positive communication leads to better outcomes. Show respect for others if you want it yourself. Admit when you are wrong. Listening is a huge part of communication -- actively listening to the other party. This means forgetting about responding – just listening and taking in what the person is actually communicating. Gosh, the things we could learn if we just absolutely and completely listened to a person.

Know your strengths and weaknesses. Be completely honest with yourself. If you are not honest with

yourself, I doubt anyone else will be honest with you. Assess yourself. Be honest with yourself. Manage yourself.

Know the difference between envy and admiration of others. Envy comes from a nasty place, and envy causes a great deal of trouble. Don't be the Green Monster of envy.

Boundaries protect us. Boundaries protect our physical space and our mental space. This leads to a decrease in stress and anxiety and moves us toward improvement in our physical and mental health. It is a great form of self-respect. Know what healthy and unhealthy boundaries are for you.

Avoid the miserable, the exceptionally unhappy. I cannot say it enough. Miserable people make everyone miserable. We have to stop these vicious cycles of negativity and misery if we are going to move toward joy!

Lastly, stop the hate. Stop condoning people who are full of hate and project that hate onto others. It is not a healthy environment AT ALL. Hate comes from a very dark place in those that are usually not as informed or educated about the things they hate as they should be. Just stop!

Embracing making ourselves a priority, remember, is not a negative thing. We must take care of ourselves in order to promote a better overall lifestyle and lead ourselves toward contentment – joy. Self-care is not a luxury. Self-care is a necessity. No one person's self-care is going to match another's because self-care is about YOU. You must discover what YOUR self-care looks like.

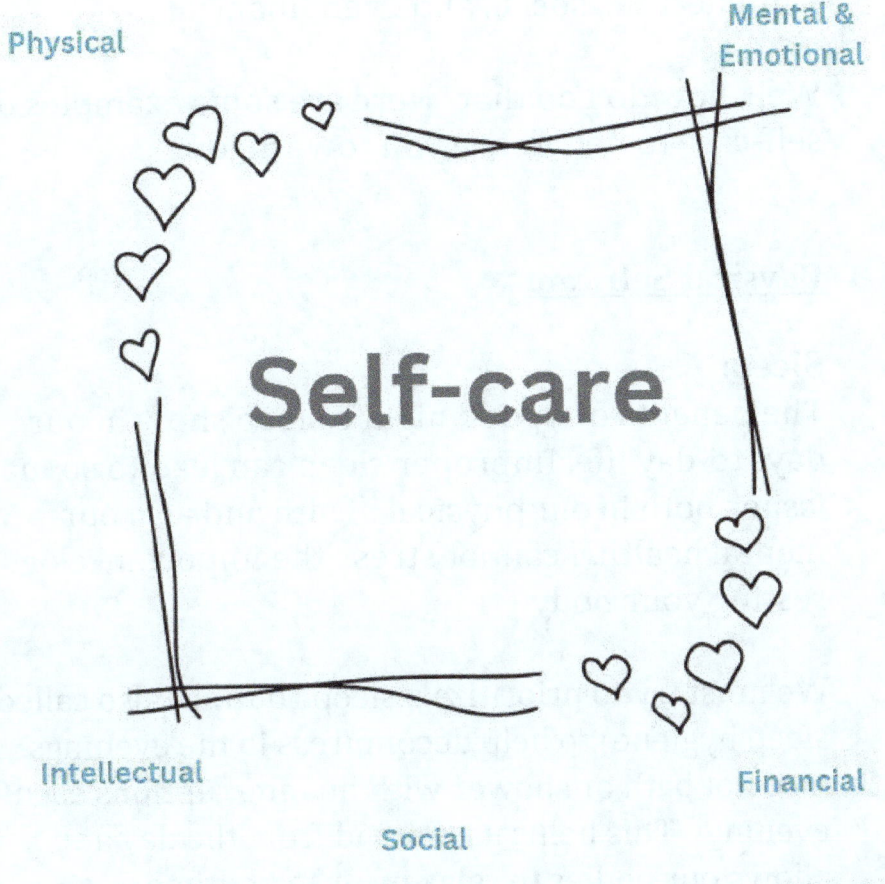

Physical

Mental & Emotional

Self-care

Intellectual

Social

Financial

Sherrie Kays 2024

Self-Care

It is not selfish to take care of ourselves. It is necessary! Forms of self-care come in the forms of whatever is beneficial to you! The types of self-care we think about most often are mental, physical, and emotional/spiritual.
There are also other ways to improve yourself.
Think of these forms of self-care to help you journal – intellectual, social, and even financial.

Well, how do I do that? Here are some examples of self-care to help move you toward joy.

Physical Self-care

Sleep:
The benefits of a good night's sleep show in our day- to-day life. Improper sleep can lead to so many issues both in our physical health and also our mental health. I cannot stress the importance of resting your body.

We must try to prioritize a sleep routine (also called sleep hygiene) to help decompress in the evenings. A nice hot bath or shower with no interruptions each evening! This helps us unwind from the day and allows our bodies to relax prior to bedtime.

Water:
Hydrate yourself. Keep a water bottle full of water all the time. When we are dehydrated, we feel it.

Nutrition:
The old saying you are what you eat is actually true. You can research all the positives and negatives of food on not only our physical bodies, but our mental health, as well.

Develop a healthier eating plan. This doesn't have to be a diet, but just regarding what we put into our bodies is important.

Activity:
You don't have to run marathons to consider yourself physically active.
Take a walk.
Make friends with nature (grounding is good for the soul).
Yoga.
Go outside and work in the flower bed. Play with a toddler.

Rest and Recharge:
Some people call this a "mental health day". I don't care what it is labeled, but there are times when we all need to rest and recharge.

Mental and Emotional Self-Care

Positive self-talk:
Make a conscious effort to be nice to yourself; negative self-talk hurts us. Talk such as: "You're never going to be able to do that." "You are not nearly as smart as she is." are not helpful to our growth.

Mindfulness or meditation:
Mindfulness or meditation helps foster awareness of the present moment, reduce stress and anxiety, and enhance mental clarity.

Journaling:
Journaling emotions, experiences, or just everyday thoughts to promote emotional well-being and a better sense of self-awareness. The feeling and why are great methods.

Relaxation and leisure:
Relaxation and leisure comes in varying forms -- deep breathing exercises, progressive muscle relaxation, or guided imagery to reduce anxiety and promote a sense of calm. Relaxation and leisure means taking time to truly relax without the television or phone distracting you. Just you. Nothing else.

Seek Support:
Seek support through trusted friends and family members. Sometimes seeking the help of a professional counselor or a therapist may be necessary to gain balance.

Intellectual Self-Care:

Always keep learning:
Listening to podcasts or watching educational videos help keep us intellectually aware.

Read and Read More

Find a hobby:
This teaches you something new. Then, keep at it. Or even better, pick up another one as long as you are balancing yourself and your time.

Social Self-Care

Boundaries: spoken of a great deal in Chapter 8.
Positive Communication: spoken of a great deal in Chapter 5.

Nurture the relationships important to YOU. Make meaningful connections with loved ones and friends who are a positive part of your life and bring positivity when you are connected.

Quality Time :with friends and loved ones, including social connection, experiences, and lots of laughter.

Financial

Identify your values:
Identify what YOU value and align your finances with these values. Don't overstretch yourself trying to "keep up with the Joneses." Is the biggest and best always good for us?

Plan your finances:
Know what you can handle financially and what you cannot. It is okay to have a smaller house if this is what your finances allow you.

Budget and manage finances accordingly:
Stay on your financial budget. A budget truly means that we can expect unexpected financial

things to come into our budget lives occasionally, and these unexpected expenses will not hurt us financially or otherwise.

Manage Debt:
This can be a tough issue because some have the mindset that everyone always has debt, and to a certain extent, this is true. However, piling up debt only decreases our overall joy because of the stress these debts are bringing to our lives.

Remember, embracing varying forms of self-care allows us to create a much more fulfilling lifestyle that overall aids in our journey toward joy. Self-care creates lasting wellness both of our physical and mental well-being.

Remember, self-care is a <u>necessity</u>, not a luxury. When we practice self-care, there is a priority established of the importance of fulfillment and satisfaction in our lives. Make the time to take care of YOU.

By exploring and experimenting with what brings you relaxation and calm, YOU are in charge of YOU. Bring on self-empowerment, purpose, and ultimately JOY.

10 Ways to Make It About <u>You</u> and Finding JOY

1. It is not your responsibility to make others happy. Their happiness is their responsibility.
2. Stop giving in to needy people – you know, the people that completely drain you both physically and mentally.
3. Know where you've been. Know where you're going.
4. Stop trying to fix everything and everyone.
5. Communicate positively.
6. Be honest with yourself. Assess yourself. Manage yourself.
7. Do not compare yourself to other people.
8. Set Boundaries and do not let those boundaries be broken by anyone.
9. Unhappy people want everyone around them to be unhappy.
10. Stop hanging around with those filled with hate.

10 Questions to Ask Ourselves

Think About These Questions for the Notes Section on Page 121

1. Am I always trying to make other people happy? Is it draining me physically, emotionally, and mentally?

2. Do I have Needy Vampires in my life? How

3. Am I honest with myself like I want others to be honest with me?

4. Am I a HAVE to x person or am I a WANT to fixer?

5. Do I use positive and effective communication? Do I truly listen to what another is saying?

6. Do I compare myself to other people in a way that takes away from my own emotional and mental well-being?

7. Do I have boundaries in my life that keep me physically, emotionally, and mentally protected?

8. Do I have miserable people in my life that I need to distance myself from?

9. Do I have people in my life that are filled with hate rather than joy?

10. How can I make a change from episodes of happiness to a more content, satisfied joy?

Visuals

Happiness	Joy
Emotion-related Usually temporary or circumstantial Externally caused	State or condition Continual, constant, long- term Internal

Sherrie Kays 2024

Joy in Other Languages

Language	Word for Joy
Spain -- Spanish	Alegría
France – French	Joie
Italy -- Italian	Gioia
Finland– Finnish	Ilo
Ireland – Irish	Áthas
Scotland – Scottish Gaelic	Gàirdeachas
Romania – Romanian	Bucurie
Greece – Greek	Χαρά
Hawaii – Hawaiian	hauʻoli
Haiti – Haitian Creole	kè kontan

Sherrie Kays 2024

CIRCLE OF CONTROL

Outside of my control – outside the circle

Others' opinions

Others' actions

Others' words

What others think of me

The future

Within My Control

My words

My actions

My mindset

My free time

Boundaries for myself

Moving on from failure and mistakes

What I give energy to

Being Present in the moment

Past Mistakes

Other people's boundaries

The outcome of my efforts

Sherrie Kays 2024

5 Points of Distance
Distance yourself from...

People who make you
question yourself

People who
make you
feel anxious

People who
drain you
mentally

People who make you
end up feeling worse
after seeing them

People who question
your WHY

Sherrie Kays 2024

Toxic Talk

I really cannot believe you would consider that.

Wait! YOU got a promotion? Wow!

If you lose some weight, you will feel so much better. I did.

I'd feel guilty if I... (finish appropriately)

I could never afford to drive a ____. How do you do it?

Toxic Feelings

Drained after talking with them

Increased stress when talking with them or immediately after

Not feeling good about yourself -- lower self-confidence and lower self-esteem

Not feeling genuinely heard during conversations with them

Feeling guilty because you do things differently or have different things than they do.

Sherrie Keys 2024

Don't forget where you came from

But never lose sight of where you are going

Sherrie Kays 2024

Oops, I Messed Up

Understand Your Mistake
Accept Your Mistake
Grieve Your Guilt
Talk to a Trusted Friend to Express Yourself
Learn from Your Mistake

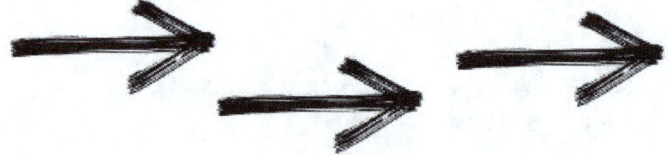

Grow from the Past
Get Away from the Shame
Get to Moving Forward -- **Deliberately**

Sherrie Kays 2024

Fixer Personalities
HAVE TO DO THIS

Overextend yourself
HAVE to feel needed
HAVE to be in control
Strong belief systems -- to a fault
NEED to fix
Don't wait for others to say "No"
NEED others to depend upon them

Fixer Personalities
WANT TO DO THIS

WANT to extend themselves to others
WANT to feel needed
Know when to relinquish control
Strong character and self-worth
WANT to fix
Accept when others say "No"
WANT others to grown and learn

Sherrie Kays 2024

Effective Communication

1. Use "I" statements
   a. "I feel needed when you ask me to help out"
   b. "I feel discouraged when you yell at me"
   c. "I need to talk to you about something that's bothering me".
2. Actively listen, reflect, and validate the family members words
3. Clarify if necessary with positive phrasing:
   a. "I'm not sure you heard what I meant. What I meant to say was..."
   b. "I am not sure I heard you correctly. Can you tell me that again?"
   c. "Did you mean...?"
4. Take responsibility for your own contribution to the misunderstanding, but do not accept all the blame for misunderstanding.
5. Inform family members of any obstacles:
   a. "I have had a really rough day, so if I am quiet/grouchy, you know why"
   b. "School did not go like I wanted it to today, so if I am anxious/stressed/grouchy, you know why"
6. Try to look for the best in your family members.
   Happy =best Unhappy=worse

Sherrie Kays 2024

Effective Communication

7. Discuss negative behaviors calmly
8. Try to let your family members know you appreciate them. Hearing "thank you" is important.
9. Let your family members know if you do not like something, so behaviors are not repeated
10. Be honest with family members. Concerns should be shared, so there is no build up, resentment, and bitterness.
11. Share concerns in a positive, respectful, constructive, caring way. Negative things are usually hard to hear, so be gentle.
12. Listen actively and with acceptance when a family member has chosen to share concerns with the family. Expressed wants and needs should not be assumed as criticism.
13. Let the family know you care about what is needed and wanted. Remember, that not everything that is needed is wanted, so agreement may not happen right away.

Sherrie Kays 2024

Effective Communication

Builds Relationship
Builds Rapport
Builds Respect

Sherrie Kays 2024

Honesty with Self

Knowledge of Weak Areas
Allowing Vulnerability
No Excuses Mindset
Seeking Guidance or Assistance in Weak Areas
Continual Improvement in Weak Areas

Dishonesty with Self

Ignorance or Oblivious of Weak Areas
Not Making Corrections to Self
Feigning Strength or Knowledge
Excuses!
Will Not Ask for Help
Weak Areas Could Worsen

Sherrie Kays 2024

Strengths Top 3 Things I am good at	**Weaknesses** Top 3 Things I need help with
1.	1.
2.	2.
3.	3.

Sherrie Kays 2024

Envy
The Green Monster

Doesn't celebrate or isn't happy when others' succeed

Judging what others do

Upset when others get praise for accomplishments

Happy when other's fail or have setbacks

Fake compliments

Trying to copy or compete with those who are the object of their envy

Spread false information or rumors

Downplays others' successes

Sherrie Kays 2024

Admiration
The Pink Pacifist

Encourages &
celebrates others'
success

Encourages others
to be better

Does not strive to
beat or compete

Happy to see
others succeed -
celebrates with
them

No drama or
falsities

Does not feed
gossip or falsities

Praises another's
accomplishments

No judgment of
others

Encourages those
who have failure or
experience set
backs

Sherrie Kays 2024

Benefits of
Boundaries

Greater autonomy and confidence
Clear expectations for others
Decreases stress and anxiety
Improves emotional health
Improves relationships
Lessens burnout
Self-respect and respect from others
Time needed for YOU

Sherrie Keys 2024

Healthy Boundaries
are not...

Emotional manipulation or guilt
tripping to get their way

Giving in because you are concerned
about hurting another's feelings

Relying on others for
sense of self-worth, meaning,
or personal identity

Invading personal space and privacy
-- lack of respect

Sherrie Keys 2024

How To Tell If a Person Is Miserable

Complaining or pointing out negative side
Unfriendly
Fishing for compliments
NEEDING others' attention
Pessimistic Attitude
Anger over the little things & showing anger
Loneliness that they may not even recognize
Feeling of hopelessness or feigning abilities
Ignoring those around them

Sherrie Kays 2024

Cycle of Misery

I have to be the best looking in the room.

Hey, I saw that dress on the clearance rack at...

Oh my gosh! Everyone is complimenting her!

Fishing for compliments and downgrading others when you don't receive the compliments wanted

Sherrie Kays 2024

Cycle of Misery

Why are her performance reviews
so much better than mine?

How in the world
do you always
get high reviews?
Are you kissing
up to the boss?

Oh my gosh! Her
ratings were high
again!
Unbelievable!

Envy of another's success and
downplaying their success

Sherrie Kays 2024

Cycle of Misery

I'm feeling awful today because
I did not take my migraine medication.

I knew you would
come and help
me feel better.

Calls on friend for
help

Gaining attention however they must and taking
advantage of others' generosity

Sherrie Kays 2024

Hatred comes from unfounded opinions of...

Age
Religion
Political Affiliation
Skin Color
Gender Identity
Sexual Orientation

Sherrie Kays 2024

Questions to Ask Ourselves

Notes Space

1. Am I always trying to make other people happy? Is it draining me physically, emotionally, and mentally?

   How can I change this if I need to?

2. Do I have Needy Vampires in my life? How can I distance myself without causing conflict?

3. Am I honest with myself like I want others to be honest with me?

How can I become more honest with myself?

4. What are my strengths and my weaknesses?

Strengths	**Weaknesses**
Top 3 Things I am good at	Top 3 Things I need help with
1.	1.
2.	2.
3.	3.

Sherrie Kays 2014

5. Do I use positive and effective communication? Do I truly listen to what another is saying?

How can I make myself a better listener?

How can I use more effective and positive communication?

6. Do I compare myself to other people in a way that takes away from my own emotional and mental well-being?

How can I stop comparing myself and protect my own well-being?

7. Do I have <u>specific</u> boundaries in my life that keep me physically, emotionally, and mentally protected?

What boundaries can I set in order to protect myself mentally and emotionally (and physically, if necessary)? List your specific boundaries here:

Specific Boundaries for Myself

8. Do I have miserable people in my life that I need to distance myself from?

How can I change this if I need to?

9.   Do I have people in my life that are filled with hate rather than joy?

How can I move toward more joy when there may be those around me filled with hate?

10. How can I make a change from episodes of
    happiness to a more content, joy-filled life?
    Make a list on the next few pages of how you can
    move deliberately toward joy in your life.

Moving Toward Joy

Author's Note:

It is quite a journey to move toward joy in your life. It is hard. It is never easy to make choices for ourselves. However, choices must be made if we are to protect our mental health, our peace, and move toward true joy.

When I first thought of a few of these chapter subjects, I had to set some aside. There are a couple of chapters that are really heavy subject matter. I'll let you determine which ones were heavy on your mind and heart. Some topics are just not easy to talk about, much less face in our daily lives.

I truly believe in JOY. Happy moments are great. I want overall satisfaction, purpose, and peace in my life. Thank you to those who help me keep my JOY.

I have tried very hard to live by these 10 subjects put forth in the book. My testimonial is that they work and have helped me live a better, more-fulfilled life of JOY.

Sherrie Kays 2024

Other Books and Journals by Sherrie Kays

Journals

The 30 Day Journal
The 30 Day Journal for Teens
The 30 Day Journal for Kids

Upcoming:
The Next 30 Days - Journal

Books upcoming

Socials Skills Adults
Missed Growing Up

Social Skills Every Child
Needs to Develop

www.ingramcontent.com/pod-product-compliance
Lightning Source LLC
Chambersburg PA
CBHW080843120626
46553CB00009B/2550